THE COMING OF THE LITTLE GREEN MAN

John Agard was born in Guyana and came to Britain in 1977. His many books include eight collections from Bloodaxe, *From the Devil's Pulpit* (1997), *Weblines* (2000), *We Brits* (2006), *Alternative Anthem: Selected Poems* (2009), *Clever Backbone* (2009), *Travel Light Travel Dark* (2013), *Playing the Ghost of Maimonides* (2016) and *The Coming of the Little Green Man* (2018). He was awarded the Queen's Gold Medal for Poetry 2012.

He won the Casa de las Américas Prize in 1982 for *Man to Pan*, a Paul Hamlyn Award in 1997, and a Cholmondeley Award in 2004. *We Brits* was shortlisted for the 2007 Decibel Writer of the Year Award, and he has won the Guyana Prize twice, first for *From the Devil's Pulpit* and then for *Weblines*.

As a touring speaker with the Commonwealth Institute, he visited nearly 2000 schools promoting Caribbean culture and poetry, and has performed on television and around the world. In 1993 he became the first Writer in Residence at London's South Bank Centre. In 1998 he was writer-in-residence for the BBC with the Windrush project, and *Bard at the Beeb*, a selection of poems written during that residency, was published by BBC Learning Support. He was writer in residence at the National Maritime Museum in Greenwich in 2007.

He is a popular children's writer whose titles include *Get Back Pimple* (Viking), *Laughter is an Egg* (Puffin), *Grandfather's Old Bruk-a-down Car* (Red Fox), *I Din Do Nuttin* (Red Fox), *Points of View with Professor Peekaboo* (Bodley Head) and *We Animals Would Like a Word with You* (Bodley Head), which won a Smarties Award. *Einstein, The Girl Who Hated Maths*, a collection inspired by mathematics, and *Hello H_2O*, a collection inspired by science, were published by Hodder Children's Books and illustrated by Satoshi Kitamura. Frances Lincoln Children's Books published his recent titles *The Young Inferno* (2008), his retelling of Dante, also illustrated by Satoshi Kitamura, which won the CLPE Poetry Award 2009, and *Goldilocks on CCTV* (2011). His first non-fiction work, *Book* (Walker Books, 2016), tells the history of books in the voice of the Book itself, and was longlisted for the 2016 Carnegie Medal.

He lives with the poet Grace Nichols and family in Sussex; they received the CLPE Poetry Award 2003 for their children's anthology *Under the Moon and Over the Sea* (Walker Books).

JOHN AGARD

The Coming of
the Little Green Man

BLOODAXE BOOKS

ISBN: 978 1 78037 418 5

First published 2018 by
Bloodaxe Books Ltd,
Eastburn,
South Park,
Hexham,
Northumberland NE46 1BS.

www.bloodaxebooks.com
For further information about Bloodaxe titles
please visit our website or write to
the above address for a catalogue.

Supported using public funding by
**ARTS COUNCIL
ENGLAND**

ACKNOWLEDGEMENTS

The poem 'A Debate' was first published in
Ploughshares (USA), Spring 2015, vol. 41 no.1

Printed in Great Britain by Bell & Bain Limited, Glasgow, Scotland, on
acid-free paper sourced from mills with FSC chain of custody certification.

*For those bibulous moments with friends who shared in
the little Green Man's evolution.*

Mark Hewitt for his as ever conspiratorial thoughts;

*William Wallis for engaging mobile-wise with
the little Green Man's odyssey among vegetables;*

*Jacob Ross for time spent journeying with
the little green arrival on a St Lucian veranda;*

*and for my poet-wife, Grace Nichols,
for casting her much-valued eye.*

CONTENTS

On our epic journey from nothing to nowhere we leave behind a trail of garments.

CEES NOOTEBOOM

Nothing to Declare

Un-jet-lagged, travelling light,
neither hero nor anti-hero,
among arrivals at Heathrow
there walked a little green man
nowhere near incognito.

Of course, airport officials
had never been prepared
for a little green arrival –
a miracle of the spectrum
with nothing to declare.

Just two luminous fingers crossed
for the sake of the cosmos.

Curtains

No apparition sprung
from a city's eye of neon

but a living
presence of unlikely hue

biding his turn
like any other in queue.

And to every rock
he was brother

and to every leaf
he was friend.

Yet the coming
of the little green man

caused something
as ordinary as curtains

to twitch.

The Way of Maps

Keeping places in their places
may be the way of maps
for guiding the lost

even at the cost
of turning borders into traps
and flags into accomplices.

The little green man follows
the true north of his nose
losing himself to find himself.

Everyday Rituals

The inter-locking
of fingers
known as handshake

the fleeting encounter
of cheek and puckered lip
known as kiss.

He's getting the hang
of everyday rituals,
though our little green man

finds rubbing noses
a more reliable prognosis
of social intercourse

between the sexes.
O how lucky the insects
with their adaptable proboscis!

Other-Heart-from-Afar

The closest expression
to foreigner in his tongue
would be *other-heart-from-afar*

so the little green man
greets each hurrying soul
like a long lost star.

See him about to high-five
a time-tight strider in pinstripe
as if it's happy hour

see him everywhere adrift
in his Buddha-green aura
the colour of a frog's back

and even as his extended
arms are side-stepped –
his familiarity frowned on

he looks beyond the bustle
to an undiscovered horizon
where every passing other

embraces each other's space
by making ample room
for what ticks below the skin.

Heart

O to discover
beat by beat

this vibrating flower
in a vase of ventricles

this throbbing fruit
in an orchard of arteries

this fluttering bell
in a cathedral of ribs

this palpitating island
in an ocean of blood

this uncharted heart
this *tierra incognita*

that casts its spell
on the human one-to-one

and makes room for angel
as well as demon.

Full of Noises

The little green man
hasn't heard of Caliban

but he knows London
to be full of noises

that colonise the ear
with a thousand twanglings

of roadworks in progress
and scrapings of skyline.

Yet that passing jet
with its carbon footprint

did not seem to hurt
and in fact gave delight

a familiar hum of home
that made him feel

he was not alone.
Sleep was hard to come by

but his inner clouds
opened like a prayer

and he whispered to himself:
Be not afeared.

Anonymous Flora

Minding the gap of course
between platform and what
the winds of change may toll

sailing staircases that billow
(better known as escalators)
in a rush-hour-swell

of distant lives made parallel
yet bound by time for
opposite horizons

feeling himself one
of a multitude
of anonymous flora

stalks of necks muffled
in sensible scarves
twigs of fingers (gloved or not)

petals of faces blooming
from private branches
and somewhere deepdown

in the frail compost of flesh
the heart's beating bulb
in need of watering.

O how beautiful
to be breathing in
a stranger's chlorophyll.

Amidst a Multitude of Vegetables

Journeying Dante-like through supermarket circles
where trolleys obey the stomach's calendar,
pausing amidst a multitude of vegetables,

the little green man sees Europe's iceberg lettuce
chilling out in diasporic proximity
to ladyfingers of sub-continental pedigree

while one slightly jet-lagged Kenyan runner bean
catches up on a wordless long-distance one-to-one
with a local shire-bred British spring onion.

And can that be broccoli from across the Channel
exchanging whispers of an edible exodus
with a desert-dreaming Peruvian asparagus?

These much-travelled recumbent ambassadors
that can bridge millennia as well as distance
for some reason keep our little green man entranced.

Lost in contemplation, he sighs: *Ah, vegetables,*
you who know how to multiply without sex,
you who seem to have no identity complex,

O you mute mentors to the globally perplexed.

The Little Green Man Eats His First Apple

Should he start by rubbing it on his sleeve,
and like Eden's first lady, Eve,
offer a forbidden half to his other half
(though, if truth be told, he has no other half?)

Should he in a moment of levity
put to the test Newton's gravity
and let the fabled fruit, gleaming blood-red,
descend on the dome of his head?

What if even the pips secrete a constellation,
holding forth a promise of life after oblivion?
Should he, like Arthur in Avalon's orchard,
feast immortal thoughts on its inner star?

If one a day keeps the doctor away, all the more
reason for a mouth to test the twinkling core.

The Little Green Man Addresses Bread

You this silent creature
scaled with all the goodness
of a wholesome crustacean crust

your hide swaddled in grain
you who will rise once again
from your hot den of slumber

to prowl a table's wilderness
and grant the famished
your daily miracle.

Instead of a Postcard

Wishing you were here beside the Thames
where bridges arch their illuminated torsos
into a metallic impression of limbo,
and sirens wail from a Babel of wheels
that would challenge even Orpheus' lyre.
Yet parables in the wind are there for free,
if you'd dare to look beyond those spires
aiming for the heavens' bull's-eye-blue
as if salvation grew from clouds
when roots are also disguised gods.

The Way Not to Go

In order to pray
the little green man
doesn't bend his knees
or look towards the skies,
for experience has taught him
that religion divides.

So the little green one
simply closes his eyes
like blind Galileo
and lets his inner firmament
show him the way
not to go.

The Speech of Monuments

1

Those dead ones still appearing on horseback,
as if armed for a pre-emptive afterlife attack,
don't acknowledge the little green man's nod.

But today finds him gazing skywards at a column
of one of posterity's departed ones.
(A must-see, according to the tourist brochure).

Here fountains salute a one-armed commander.
The perfect spot for a photo op
after you've shopped till you dropped.

The little green man hasn't heard of Waterloo,
for where he comes from warfare is taboo.
Not easy finding a word for battalion

once you've seen the lamb lie down with the lion.
At least, here the pigeons don't seem at all fussed
by a little tourist the colour of asparagus.

2

what language do they actually speak
these unblinking sentinels of bronze

keeping a monumental eye
on how the living breathe and move?

Horse, chariot, sword, lance, mitre, crown,
all in superior suspension.

But for the little green man now lost
in the labyrinth of an *A to Z*

these Titan keepers of the past
(especially in the dark)

can sometimes serve the present
as a very handy landmark.

That still doesn't answer the question:
what language do monuments speak?

The pigeons answer with a telling beak.

Daring to Cross

According to the law of optics
green is the easiest colour
for the human eye to perceive
(hence the go-ahead green
ingrained in traffic lights).
But not wishing to incite
swear words or swear fingers
into apocalyptic road rage,
our little green man lingers
for what seems an age
before daring to cross
himself at the crossing.

A Case of Mistaken Identity

In a world of the plural
being green keeps one singular.
Not much chance of a tap on the shoulder
because you're mistaken for some *Other*.

The Little Green Man Meets the Press

Would it be politcally incorrect to address
you as 'greenie?'

We say of all green types,
the people who are not yet ripe.

How does it feel to be an ethnic
minority of one?

I have many trees for allies
and so feel mutiplied.

A Debate

A black man and a white man
like two philosophical mates
are engaged in a debate.

What has only one syllable,
no eye, no ear, no tongue,
yet is God's class act creation?

Night, says the black man.
It has to be night
that inspires rest and mystery.

Day, says the white man.
It has to be day
that announces the sun's glory.

Grass, says the little green man,
adding his bit to the debate.
Grass must be God's masterpiece.

Grass? laugh the others
who fancied themselves scholars.
A masterpiece to be trodden on!

Grass, repeats the little green man.
A sun bed for the living.
A duvet for the dead.

Ticking Boxes

Ethnic monitoring is proving problematic.
Which little box should the little green man tick?

He hesitates to tick *Chinese* (not with his skin)
even if he can show proof of his yang and yin.

Eastern European   might be worth a try.
O to be throat-singing under a Bulgarian sky!

White Other   offers some leeway for manoeuvre.
Maybe he'll meet his genetic match in Dover.

Afro-Caribbean   sounds sunshinely syncopated
but he draws the line at being hyphenated.

Alien   has a certain otherworldly ring.
Makes you feel every planet is your sibling.

But it's hard work, pruning one's family tree,
when one's roots reach for distant galaxies.

He concludes that questionnaires are enhanced
when little boxes break into their global dance.

Embracing Glorious Uncertainty

See how the little green man blends
in with the tea-calm village green
under a tentative summer sky.

Glorious uncertainty can be so serene,
indeed almost atavistically benign,
causing him to feel within his deeps
how the wielded willow still weeps
for the cow's sacrifice of hide
to the red meteor of leather.

Witness a tribe of white-flannelled
devotees of Judgement's fair finger.
And what are those three sentinels for?
Upright as Fate's grim messengers,
holding past present future
under the fragile bails of time.

And who in heaven's name can that be
behind the stumps of destiny
like the uninvited thirteenth fairy?

Surely not a little green intruder
squatting like a woman giving birth.

Breaking the Ice

'Don't you just hate this weather?'
locals would ask the little green man with a sigh,
on hearing of brute force thunder prophesied.

Oh, he replies, *don't you just love it*
when old Papa Thunder beats his divine drum
and Noah's nemesis comes pissing down?

Where did he learn such quaint English
is a question that crosses their mind,
but it wouldn't be the done thing to pry.

And when snow comes to surprise mid-August,
resigned faces give rise to moaning outbursts:
'Freak snow! Now that's all we bloody need!'

But the little green man exclaims with glee:
Mama Sky is so house proud, it must be said.
There she goes shaking out her feather bed!

Attuned to the clouds' shape-shifting choreography,
(meteorologically speaking, the odd one out)
he'd give the elements the benefit of the doubt.

But when two strangers share their inner weather
the little green man finds such moments o-so-nice.
Maybe this is what's meant by breaking the ice.

Overnight Shampoo

In the mirror of morning light,
the little green man wakes to find
the trees have had an overnight
shampoo of unscheduled snow –

leaves turn to ice-beaded braids
and frosty perms and white afros
re-style yesterday's shrub.

God mst be a hairdresser.
Bless him, bless her, whatever.

Throwing Caution

When the fingers of frost
turn morning's leaves
to crystal lobes

and blades
of dew-glazed grass
to trodden-on gems

and the ducks ripple
a pond's surface into
a revolving necklace

and a sky of slate
surprises the head
with jewels of hail

our little green man
feels rich enough
to throw caution

to proverbial winds.
No looking
over his shoulder

for a flash of steel.

Bookworm

The little green man likes
to keep his nose
in nature's book.

So he peruses
the pages of a rose
skimming thorns of punctuation

the paragraphs of grass
the rolling chapters of ocean
that glue him to their saga.

And curled up at bedtime
with night's encyclopedia
he thumbs the sky's soft spine

browsing the volumes of stars
for a morsel of insight
like God's little bookworm.

A Bonsai Moment

Bonsai tree
sprouting from a dish,
whenever I water you
I make a little wish.

Bonsai, like me,
you've come from afar.
Let me see you twinkle
O tree of a thousand stars.

The Little Green Man Goes Pub Crawling

Of course he could have gone
to the *Fox and Hound*
the *George and Dragon*
the *Blade and Bone*
the Bleeding Wolf
the *Horse and Knacker*
the *Hung Drawn and Quartered*
the *Cat and Canary*

but being wary
of any whiff of confrontation
(even of the verbally unintentional kind)

he settles for the settling sign
that says simply the *Green Man*
with a figure in leafy jerkin
who could pass for his own kin.

Ah well, he's a long way from home
but wherever he lays his atoms
that's his genome.

Six Takes on the Little Green Man

Surgeon:
We've seen albinos, but green skin is a one-off.
Gentlemen, a genetic breakthrough awaits.
Be sure to get his DNA before he assimilates.

Linguist:
There are word-gems lurking in his gutturals.
Indeed, his speech sounds almost oracular.
He'll lend colour to our vernacular.

TV Producer:
Our little green man can be the new Parkinson.
Telly opens doors to every pigmentation.
His own chat show will be a prime-time sensation.

Gardener:
Rumour has it his touch revives a drooping rose.
His green fingers are digits that beguile.
Plants don't seem to mind a refugee or exile.

Politician:
Who better to front our eco-manifesto?
Whatever his creed or sexual bent,
he can be spokesperson for the environment.

Cosmetician:
Green isn't what you'd call a normal skin tone.
But our advanced serums work wonders.
Guaranteed to remove all trace of borders.

Beware of the Door!

Because the little green
is the only one
on his street without a dog

and not wanting to bring down
the neighbourhood's tone
he decides to erect a sign –

BEWARE OF THE DOOR!
The neighbours sigh, he's foreign,
forgive his spelling.

But if truth be told,
the little green man is sensing
there's nothing to fear from a dog

providing of course
the dog maintains its place
on the right side of the door

and is happy to chew on
a bone that's not your own.
No, it's the door that poses a threat

for doors can't be trained to fetch
or promise to be Man's best friend.
No, doors promise only a step

of faith into the unknown –
a covenant with a threshold
where mindsets are put to the test.

Meeting Hedgehog

Bloody pest!
says neighbour to left.

Breeds termites!
says neighbour to right.

In this manner two suburbanites
introduce the little green man
to his first hedgehog.

And bending towards
the unmoving dome of spines,
he greets the bristling one.

The pleasure is mine, all mine,
O little prickly poet-in-residence.

Getting It Politically Correct

Are those black
or non-white clouds
gathered in a huddle?

Is that white
or non-black snow
waiting to be shovelled?

The little green man
keeps such questions
to himself

preferring to jump
the fences of language
on ladders of love

not wanting to choose
between the non-white raven
and the non-black dove.

Letter to the Lexicographer

Dear Lexicographer

what makes you so sure that the monster
which goes by the name of jealousy
can be defined as green-eyed?

Does a tree, content in its throne of bark,
envy the moon its golden stride?

Does a blade of grass go ballistic
when flowers flaunt their brazen palette?

Does a leaf tremble with resentment
when the sunset poses in its flaming finery?

   O dearie me dearie me
who was it that dubbed it a drudgery
    this business of lexicography?

     Yours Sincerely
     Little Green-Eyed

Algebra of the Epidermis

Assuming that shades combine *ad infinitum*
within a given ancestral closet of copulation

let X, for starters, be the unknown
little gnome (or should that be genome?)

or to put it another way, let X,
in the wheel of the human equation,
represent the heart's unpredictable spoke

or maybe a case of the co-efficient gods
having a superior private joke

forever multiplying and dividing the genetic loaf
into a constant miracle of inconstant slices
thereby precipitating the purest of purists

towards an unsolvable epidermal crisis.
But who gives a fraction?

Patriot or Not

That flag
of flame
hoisting itself
from a candle's pole
demands no salute
fom a bleeding moon
or that the trees
stand to attention.
And in the name
of night's anthem
the little green man
would gladly surrender
to an army of stars
and follow blindly
a candle's
flickering banner.

The Little Green Man Addresses a Leaf

Spring's
new-sprung
earring

veined
no less

than human
flesh.

Keeping Abreast of a Stone

Stone, how do you manage to sit so still
when there's so much going on in the world?

Is it because stones don't read newspapers?
Is it because stones don't squat in front of tv

and therefore out of touch with the latest
in bombings, crashes, fires, quakes, tsunamis?

For an answer the little green man leans closer
towards the wrinkly earlobe of a stone

that nestled in his palm like an orphaned foetus
(small but perfectly formed, as the saying goes).

But not a stone you'd find in your guidebook.
Not a stone you'd want to write home about.

Not exactly the stone Jacob used for a pillow
not the black stone Muslim pilgrims yearn to kiss

nor the one of destiny in Westminster Abbey
on which British bluebloods take a sovereign's seat.

No, just a common little stone that finds its way
into the unsuspecting heel of a shoe

or one the prankish hand of a child might salvage
for hurling even at nothing that moves.

Yet, to a green ear, a mute stone speaks volumes
when the heavens let fall their mineral teardrops.

Question Time Is Running Out of Time, So One Final Question from the Little Green Gentleman in the Back Row

With hunger's eyes of melting marble
beseeching an invisible global table,
and the echo of rubble in the bone,
would the Panel care to explain,
in the light of so much breaking news
bearing witness by remote control
to the silent gestures of the broken,
how does the heart find a way to stay whole?

I'm afraid that's all we have time for. Thank you for watching
Question Time.

Not Lost in Translation

Because he has learnt
from the book of autumn

he sees in every face
a human leaf

falling from the tree
of laughter and grief

and because laughter
needs no passport

and grief no country
of origin

the little green man
concludes that tears

require no sub-titles
to translate

their transparent tracks
those pearly drops

of broken glass
enough to prove

how a flesh-and-blood
mirror cracks.

On the Button

Doesn't take long

for an earthquake
to make a relic
of a civilisation

for a volcano
to consign a town
to oblivion

for a mudslide
to erase
a village

not to mention freak floods
killer droughts
the hurricane ache
you name it.

So why the need for weapons
of mass apocalypse
when mother nature
only has to shrug her hips?

Time for the little green man
to ask a silly question:

Does pressing a button
make men feel the masters
of their own disasters?

Looking on the Green Side

To lean towards the glass that beckons
a half-full horizon

to see a glint of spring in a snowflake's
fleeting geometry

to hear the soft decibels of roots and leaves
coming into being

even to marvel at how the weeds mourn
hoisting their half-mast green

over collateral flesh and bone.

Keen to Give Blood

The little green man is keen to give blood –
do his bit for blood-spilling humankind.
And a prick in the arm is a small price to pay
for staying grounded in the mortal mind.

But what if earth folks would settle for a coma
rather than plasma from a little green donor?
He is reassured by the smiling nurse
that he's a progressive step for transfusion.

Yet knowing blood to be both blessing and curse,
she labels his red pint green to avoid confusion.

The Little Green Man at Carnival

Carnival
is a beautiful
time to be green

in a topsy-turvy
multi-colour
of abandon

when Notting Hill
forsakes hierarchy
for foolery.

Whoever is not foolish
at Carnival
is foolish all year round

says the German proverb.
Now on London's
Blitz-bred ground

old Europe
lets its hybrid
hair down.

The Little Green Man Goes on a Blind Date

1

Tonight the little green man
is seated at a table for two
in a candle-lit rendezvous
with a never-met companion.
But all things are possible.
If not an exchange of soul atoms,
then perhaps the small miracle
of random digits daring
to risk an amicable pairing.
Can that be old Pythagoras
pouring Bacchus into a wine glass?

2

When a stranger's eyes reveal heaven's spheres,
this *tierra incognita* can feel like a prelude to prayer.
O how blessed to be in the company of one
who thinks of herself as a night person.
She who perks up with the evening primrose.
She who translates the tongue of ivy and oak.
At her best in the light of chameleon shadows.

And a night like this stays forever young
when the heart's abandon begins to rule
and wisdom follows the way of the fool.

3

'I've never been with a little green man,
but I'll try anything for the sake of the planet,'
she said, revealing the small rainforest
preserved in her armpit
like the very lungs of Eden.

'And I've never been with a flesh-and-blood
epiphany,' he said, feeling
the globe of himself spinning on her axis.
Boundaries dissolving without a kiss.
Global warming without the risk.

4

Curiosity they say
killed the cat
but keeps alive

the feline
in strangers
feeling to purr

and exercise their paws
pursue the awe
of an eyeball's meteor

discover hidden whiskers
in their own milky way
rub against each other's

furniture of skin on skin
not thinking whether
or not the earth had moved

yet in their porous depths
a sort of seismic shift –
an eclipse of self and self.

Misgivings from the Far Right

Interracial sex is one thing.
Not that we're for the colour bar.
But isn't intergalactic
intercourse going a bit too far?

The Little Green Man's Nativity

Once more into the human zone
to feel his emerald self

blossom into flesh and bone
amidst December's festive babble.

No need for mistletoe
to feel as vulnerable

as Balder the beautiful
in this season known as merry.

Peace and goodwill to the one
who by holly is restored

when weeping eyes shed their berries
and love shows evil the door.

Thought for the Day

From the grasshopper's genuflection
at a tabernacle of grass

from the snail's pilgrim trail
complete with its temple of a shell

from the bats' monkish huddle
into the sanctuary of themselves

from the birds on Ascension wings
chorussing their hosannas

from the moon's crescent footsteps
towards the Mecca of itself

from the wind scattering its gospel
from a leaf's response to the good news

the little green man pauses to reflect:
so many bounties heaped on one planet!

And The Word Was Made Flesh

If in the Beginning was the Word,
would it be cheeky to ask what colour
was the Beginning and the Word?

Still the little green man will sing
in praise of the dark void
that sprouted into word-embryos

until that common gift, the tongue,
blessed with guttural *ahhhs!* and *ohhhs!*
discovered flesh in an evergreen noun.

Witness

This olive tree remembers
a dove returning to an ark.
A long forgotten flood.

This olive tree bears the mark
of a prophet's blood
that flowered into text.

This olive tree feeds the spark
that keeps the heart's lamp
burning to be blessed.

This olive tree is neither
of the East nor of the West –
anointing all the broken.

But who will heed these words
a little green man
has spoken?